MW00460488

IMAGES
of America

VICKSBURG

Stepping stones made it easier to cross muddy China Street when this photo was taken in 1876. Up the hill from the Stonewall Exchange, on the right, was 1500 China Street, a house of ill repute that was nationally famous. (HJH.)

Cover Photograph: People crowded the terraces of the Warren County Court House in October 1907 to hear Pres. Theodore Roosevelt when J. Mack Moore took this picture. In 1948, the abandoned building became the Old Court House Museum; in later years, the name of the museum's founder, Eva W. Davis, was added. The building, located at 1008 Cherry Street, is the headquarters for the Vicksburg and Warren County Historical Society.

IMAGES
of America

VICKSBURG

Gordon A. Cotton

ARCADIA

Copyright © 1999 by Gordon A. Cotton.
ISBN 0-7385-0155-7

Published by Arcadia Publishing,
an imprint of Tempus Publishing, Inc.
2 Cumberland Street
Charleston, SC 29401

Printed in Great Britain.

Library of Congress Catalog Card Number: 99-61641

For all general information contact Arcadia Publishing at:
Telephone 843-853-2070
Fax 843-853-0044
E-Mail arcadia@charleston.net

For customer service and orders:
Toll-Free 1-888-313-BOOK

Visit us on the internet at http://www.arcadiaimages.com

Acknowledgments

Most of the pictures in this volume are from the collection of the Old Court House Museum. The earliest ones, dating from 1876, were taken by Vicksburg photographer Henry J. Herrick, who was a Canadian and a Confederate Veteran. Throughout the text, certain images are followed with these photo credits: Henry J. Herrick (HJH); Abner Blanks (AB); J. Mack Moore (JMM); Charlie Faulk (CF); Joseph B. Unglaub (JBU); Annie Lee Guider (ALG); Judson Purvis (JP); Ryland Rudd (RR); Gordon Cotton (GC); Eva W. Davis (EWD); Ken Parks (KP); J.N. Hillhouse (JNH); Bette E. Barber (BEB); and Henry J. Rhodes (HJR). If there is not a notation, the identity of the photographer is unknown.

Copies of the photos taken by Herrick, Blanks, and Moore are available by contacting the Curator, Old Court House Museum, 1008 Cherry Street, Vicksburg, Miss., 39183.

The assistance of Jeff T. Giambrone of the staff at the Old Court House Museum was invaluable in producing this book.

CONTENTS

Introduction   6

1.   All Around the Town   9

2.   When Cotton was King   63

3.   Eras of Steam & Steel   71

4.   A Tribute to Valor   81

5.   Tragedies & Tribulations   91

6.   Remembering the Good Times   101

7.   A Visit to the Country   115

INTRODUCTION

Vicksburg, Mississippi, was born of the river. It was no accident that Rev. Newet Vick chose the bluffs overlooking an S-shaped curve of the Mississippi River for the site of his town in 1819. Unlike earlier settlements, such as Warrenton a few miles to the south, Vicksburg proper would be free from the overflow of unpredictable flood waters.

Vick wasn't the first to appear on the bluffs and envision a city. Over a century earlier and about 10 miles north, a French priest had established an outpost in 1698, the oldest European settlement in what was to become Mississippi. He called it St. Pierre. The French government sent settlers—about 400—and soldiers, but the area reverted to wilderness after a massacre in 1730.

In the 1760s, during English dominion, a few land grants were made along the Mississippi near its confluence with the Big Black. In the area where Vicksburg would one day be established lived a man named Dayton, who lost his frontier holdings to a flatboat of Americans making their way down river to New Orleans, looting and pillaging as they went. It was the area's first brush with the American Revolution.

When the Spanish first saw the tree-covered bluffs, they gave them a name—Nogales—but the Tories who came to escape the revolution, to inhabit the Fourteenth Colony and hold it for His Royal Majesty, anglicized the foreign-sounding word to "Walnut Hills." In 1798, the Americans raised the Stars and Stripes over the hills, and newcomers from the eastern seaboard began a steady migration, first clearing small plots, then larger ones, until fields stretched far into the distance. The view from a hundred hills, as novelist Howard Breslin later called it, was spectacular.

Two South Carolinians, Robert Turnbull and Elihu Hall Bay, viewed the site and contemplated a town, but it was the Methodist preacher with a vision who went ahead with the plans and gave his name to the new burg. He and his wife died of yellow fever less than an hour apart on the same day in 1819; it would be up to others to nurture the town's growth.

It grew rapidly. The brown, rushing waters that washed its doorstep and the river over which canoes had once peacefully glided became the highway of mid-America. It brought the rowdy frontiersmen who tied up their flatboats beside the muddy banks, mixing the wild mint along the bayou with their whiskey. They danced and drank and brawled in the shanties that catered to their instincts. Another type vessel that resembled a floating wedding cake (or so Mark Twain thought), ushered into the Vicksburg scene a new era; steamboats brought a different class of people, many who came not so much for a fast fortune as for a permanent home. In time, scattered farms evolved into plantations, small trading posts became mercantile establishments, modest homes were expanded to elegant mansions that lined the terraced hills, and Vicksburg took its place with the cultured cities of the South.

In 1863, Vicksburg kept a rendezvous with history and left its name indelibly imprinted upon its pages. Her political sentiments had been for the preservation of the Union, but few places would pay a higher price for a role in the Confederate States than did Vicksburg. She was as strategically located for war as Vick had envisioned the site in times of peace. When the smoke had cleared, after months of fighting and 47 days of siege, the city was scarred and wounded and subdued, but her spirit was never conquered.

From the ruins and from the ashes, Vicksburg rebuilt and entered the era of the New South with determined confidence. By 1876, at the end of military occupation, there were few physical blemishes remaining from the war, and Vicksburg began an era of boom and bustle and financial revival. Its prosperity was measured through construction.

The pulse of the city, though, was along the waterfront, or Catfish Row, as David Cohn called it in later years. Here were mixed the fog-horn blast of a steamboat's whistle, the chug-chug-chug of a train engine, the songs and banter of roustabouts loading cotton, or the gaiety and foolish laughter that emanated from the shanties where you could buy fish and chips and home brew, or even lusty pleasures.

In April 1876, Vicksburgers awakened to discover that, overnight, the river had moved away from their door, taking a shorter route south; much of the city's business also moved downstream a mile or two, to Kleinston. The river that had given rise to Vicksburg now threatened to be the death of the city. It would be a quarter of a century or more before the old river was dredged, a channel dug, and the waters of the Yazoo diverted to the city front.

The city was small, but it was the largest in the state until the early 1900s. Yet it had a cosmopolitan air. The most famous names in theater gave routine performances in the elegant opera house on Walnut Street, and an electric trolley system made travel to almost any part of the city easily accessible. The city had electricity in the 1870s, telephones in the 1880s, and the tallest building in the state in 1907. The *Herald* was the only newspaper in the state with telegraphic news service, and WQBC was the oldest radio station in Mississippi. The Vicksburg Billies, a semi-pro team, were the pride of sports fans and the baseball diamond.

Celebrities had always stopped for visits in the river city, and in the years after the war, Vicksburg hosted such personalities as the Grand Duke Alexis of Russia, Emperor Dom Pedro II of Brazil, British actor Oscar Wilde, American suffragette Carrie Chapman Catt, black educator Booker T. Washington, former president U.S. Grant, Emon deValera (who was the first president of Ireland), and three of our nation's chief executives—William McKinley, Theodore Roosevelt, and William Howard Taft. Another visitor, a general who would be president, was Dwight D. Eisenhower.

Vicksburg and Warren County were also home to many who made history, the list being headed by Jefferson Davis, the only president of the Confederate States. Others included Key Pittman, a senator from Nevada, and William Gwin, the first senator from California. An early governor of California was John Downey, who was also from Vicksburg. Others who once called the city home were Confederate generals Richard Griffith and Nathaniel Harris and authors Josiah Gilbert Holland and Harris Dixon. Three chief justices of the state's supreme court, William Lewis Sharkey, Alexander Montgomery, and Horatio Fleming Simrall, also had Warren County addresses. The first black United States senator, Hiram G. Revels, lived in Vicksburg, and Joseph Holt, judge advocate general for Abraham Lincoln, had been a Vicksburg lawyer. Sarah Breedlove Walker, born across the river in Madison Parish, lived in Vicksburg as a young lady; she would go on to other places and earn a place in history as the first black female multimillionaire in the United States.

Vicksburg boasted of it firsts, including the first place Coca-Cola was bottled for sale, the first shoe store that paired its shoes and sold them in boxes, the home of the first female rural mail carrier in the country, the first Jewish synagogue, the first Eastern Orthodox church, and the first Seventh Day Adventist church in the state. The musical term "jazz" originated in Vicksburg as did the mint julep. In this city, the first Christmas tree in the state was erected in 1851.

War put the name of Vicksburg on the map, and the heroism of the era was commemorated with a national cemetery, a national military park, and the Confederate cemetery. The establishment of the Waterways Experiment Station and the lower division of the Mississippi River Commission also helped shape the city's history and mold her character.

In some instances, Vicksburg stubbornly held onto her past. The city surrendered on July 4, 1863, and the hurt lasted for generations. It was 1945 before Independence Day was celebrated in a spirit of thanksgiving that World War II was coming to an end. Even then, reluctant citizens called the festivities "The Carnival of the Confederacy."

A modern city today, Vicksburg still has areas of shady, tree-lined brick streets and architectural gems. Standing on one of the highest hills in town is the Old Court House, a magnificent structure where so much history happened. For almost 140 years, its cupola has dominated the horizon and pierced the skyline. Proudly it stands, the symbol of Vicksburg.

The spire of St. Paul Catholic Church breaks the skyline on this 1876 photo, which shows numerous business signs along the hillside and the Grangers' Hotel and Boarding House on Levee Street in the foreground. (HJH.)

One

ALL AROUND THE TOWN

For a few cents, Vicksburg offered the best entertainment and the most fun for the money. In the 1920s, for example, you could buy a trolley ticket and ride all over town for 7¢, then get a transfer and ride some more. You could dance all the way to Louisiana and back, all day long, for a quarter, or you could just relax on the deck of the Mississippi River ferry, enjoy the band music, and while away the hours.

There were places to go and things to see. There were plays at the opera house, ice cream at Berdon's, and lunch at the Elite (that's pronounced E-light) Cafe. It was fun to take an afternoon ride looking at new houses, checking out the changes, or seeing who else might be out and about.

There had been a time, in the 1880s and later, when cattle grazed all over town; there was at least one cistern in every yard, and most houses had outdoor toilets. There were neat cabins, rundown shacks, and shantyboats tied to the willows on the waterfront. The city also had its share of beautiful homes and churches. An abundance of houses featured distinctive, pierced front porch columns, an architectural feature found in few other cities.

In many respects, life was pretty routine, with church bells ringing, trolleys running on time, folks going to work or school, and the *Post* on the street by noon. Occasionally, however, a car would start down the Clay Street hill, its brakes would fail, and it would wind up submerged in the canal.

Washington Street, shown here looking north from Crawford, was the busiest part of town in the 1920s. (JMM.)

Walker Brooke, a United States senator and Confederate congressman, lived in this home on the corner of Cherry and South Streets. It was later torn down and the First Presbyterian Church was built on the site. Brooke choked to death on a raw oyster in 1869. (JMM.)

Looking east on Crawford Street in 1947, the photographer captured part of the Catholic and Baptist churches (left). On the right is city hall, the post office, Street Clinic and Mercy Hospital, and the tower of the Methodist church. (CF.)

Shown here, surrounded by 50-pound watermelons that he grew himself, is Newton Cooper. Known as "The Watermelon Man," the Confederate veteran grew some much larger than these. Selling the seeds was a profitable business. (JMM.)

This Confederate nine-inch Dahlgren was discarded for years before Joe Gerache Sr. bought it and had it mounted in the middle of Washington Street, in front of his drugstore. The man (hardly visible) reading the *Commercial-Herald* is Peter Forbus.

An outdoor baptismal service was held in in Vicksburg *c.* 1900, in what appears to be a dammed-up creek. This was apparently done to make the water deep enough for immersion. It wasn't raining; the umbrellas were used to shield the sun. (JMM.)

In this *c.* 1919 view, the snow that covered Vicksburg left white frosting on the roof and parapets of Holy Trinity Church.

The interior of Holy Trinity Church, Episcopal, includes some Tiffany windows. (JMM.)

"Shamrock," the home of the Porterfields, stood where the railroad separates Mulberry and Oak Streets. Though it was damaged in the siege in 1863, it survived until 1936. It was demolished that year. (JMM.)

In the 1960s and early 1970s, information for tourists was dispensed from this tiny building. It was located at the intersection of Monroe Boulevard and Clay. (CF.)

Pleasant Green M.B. Church hosted a meeting with Dr. Martin Luther King Jr. as speaker in the 1960s. The date of photograph, which was taken much earlier, is unknown. (JMM.)

The antebellum Willis home stood on Cherry Street facing north, but after Mrs. Willis's brother built a home on the corner, she added the circular porch, giving the house a Cherry Street entrance. A service station, shops, and a warehouse are now located on the site. (JMM.)

The Butts house, built after the War Between the States, was on the corner of Cherry and South. It was razed in the 1950s and is now the site of the Cashman Building. (JMM.)

Chickens cluster around the porch as if anticipating feeding time at this unpretentious cabin. (JMM.)

Despite his ragged clothing, the older gentleman pictured above has a certain air of dignity. (JMM.)

The Cassell Drug Company stood on the corner of Clay and Washington Streets. It was later Chilton Drug Company and in the mid-1900s was a dry cleaners. Note the iron balconies on the side. (JMM.)

This home stood just east of the convent on the corner of Crawford and Adams Streets and was similar in design to others in that area built in the 1830s. Cattle ranged freely throughout the city when this picture was taken in 1876. (HJH.)

The city hall and market place stood in the middle of Monroe Boulevard. It appears ramshackle in this photo from 1900, but it was strong enough to withstand an earthquake in the 1880s. (JMM.)

Mr. and Mrs. Philip Sartorius observed their 50th wedding anniversary in 1911. Sartorius, a merchant, moved to the area from Germany when he was a boy and operated stores in Louisiana and Mississippi. He was the first Confederate soldier wounded in the Vicksburg campaign of 1863. (JMM.)

The Jewish temple on Cherry Street is shown here, near the top of this 1876 photo. There was a pond down the hill, at the corner of Clay and Monroe. From the 1820s until 1840, Vicksburg Jews worshipped in private homes. The synagogue was built in 1870. (HJH.)

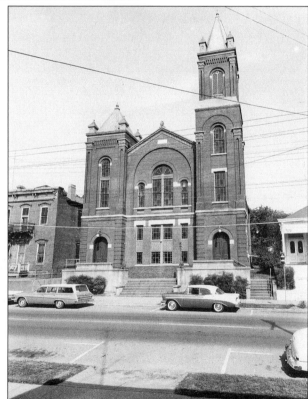

Twin towers and a new entrance foyer were added to the Jewish temple, probably around the turn of the century. The congregation, Anshe Chesed, was organized in 1842 and chartered in 1862. The building was demolished after a new temple was built in 1969.

The day this photo was taken in north Vicksburg was a wet, cold, and dreary one. Note the toilets in the back yards of the shotgun houses. (JMM.)

A view of the city from near Glass Bayou, north of town, shows the Yazoo Canal, DeSoto Island, Delta Point, and Lake Centennial in the early 1900s. (JMM.)

Christ Episcopal Church was organized in 1828 and the cornerstone was placed in 1839. The building suffered extensive damage during the siege, and following the surrender of the city, several ladies walked out when a northern-born priest prayed for Abe Lincoln rather than Jefferson Davis. In later years, stucco was applied to the brick building.

Major Charles Swett was wearing his Confederate reunion ribbons and holding his sword when he posed for this photo. He had been commander of Swett's Battery. (JMM.)

Tom Wince stands beside the star that marked the entrance to The Blue Room, an internationally famous night club that he operated on Clay Street in the mid-1900s. (GC.)

Porter Brothers Garage on Walnut Street, located beside city hall, later housed Neill's Garage, then the White Store, and federal government offices before it was bought by the City for office space. (JMM.)

The Cowan home on Cherry Street was outside the city limits when it was built before the War Between the States. It is presently Fisher-Riles Funeral Home. The photo was probably taken in 1919. (JMM.)

Dry goods have replaced fruits and vegetables, and antiques have taken their place for sale at the southwest corner of Washington and South Streets. Soon after this photo was taken, J.C. Penney built on the site. It is now an antique shop.

Can-Can cuties entertain at a production of "Gold in the Hills," a melodrama produced seasonally in Vicksburg since the 1930s. (RR.)

Lucy Arcaro sings in the bowery scene from "Gold in the Hills." The play is listed in the *Guinness Book of World Records* as the longest-running melodrama. (RR.)

The first monument to the Confederate soldiers dedicated in Vicksburg was on June 11, 1887. It was paid for by Louisiana veterans of the siege. In the background is Holy Trinity Church and the Raworth home. (JMM.)

When John Alexander Klein built Cedar Grove in the 1840s and 1850s, the lawn of the mansion extended to the Mississippi River some quarter mile or more away. Several small cannon balls, from the bombardment of 1862, are imbedded in the walls. (JMM.)

In 1855, Presbyterians built the sanctuary at the corner of Walnut and Clay Streets where The Vicksburg is located today. The church burned in 1908, on the day the congregation moved into their new sanctuary on South and Cherry Streets. (HJH.)

The convent for the Sisters of Mercy, located on Crawford Street, was built in 1868. This photo was taken in 1876. (HJH.)

The occasion was probably Robert E. Lee's birthday (January 19). A portrait of him is displayed on the right and a bust is on the left (partially hidden by the flag). The elderly man is Louis Hornthal, Vicksburg's last remaining Confederate veteran. He died in 1939.

Steamboats, trains, and people crowded the waterfront when this photo was taken in 1916. (JMM.)

In 1948, Eva Whitaker Davis opened the doors of the Old Court House as a museum. For months before that time, she spent countless hours cleaning the rooms and sorting through the debris. (CF.)

In 1876, a marble yard was located across the street from the courthouse, with displays making it look like a cemetery. The people are unidentified. (HJH.)

John Beauregard Lee was photographed washing his taxi, probably shortly before his death in February 1916. He was killed when his car overturned on Warrenton Road. He and his brother Eaton Lee owned and operated Lee Brothers Livery Stable before the advent of the automobile.

Built in the mid-1830s by John Bobb, a professional builder, the Cowan home on Crawford Street later served as headquarters for Gen. John C. Pemberton during the siege. The front porch was a later addition. Note the brick sidewalk and the dirt street in this early 1900s view. (JMM.)

The Hardaway Home on Cherry Street was built in 1850, just outside the city limits. Also known as the Gamble house and the McCabe house, it was featured in the film *The Crisis* in 1916. It was later demolished and Carr Central High School was built on the site. (JMM.)

Built in 1897 on the corner of Cherry and Grove Streets, McInerney's Hall and Confectionery occupied the former site of the Hill City Marble Company, opposite the Old Court House. In the 1920s, it was called the Halpin Building. When it was demolished in 1939 to make way for the new courthouse, it was the Liberty Cash Grocery. (JMM.)

Known in recent years as Planter's Hall, this building on the northwest corner of Main and Monroe Streets was built in the early 1830s as a bank. For a number of years, in the mid-1900s, it was the headquarters for the Vicksburg Council of Garden Clubs. The picture was taken c. 1917. (JMM.)

The first B'Nai B'rith Literary Association building was erected in 1892 on the corner of Clay and Walnut Streets. The structure burned May 19, 1915. The club was organized in 1887, with Joe Hirsch as president. (JMM.)

The Railroad and Commercial Bank on the corner of Jackson and Cherry Streets was chartered in 1833 and was expected to finance the construction of a railroad line between Vicksburg and Jackson. Though the bank failed in 1839, the building stood until it was destroyed by a tornado in 1953. In the background is the old Steigleman home. (HJH.)

In the years immediately after the War Between the States, George H. Dorsey operated a harness and saddle shop at the corner of Clay and Washington Streets. In 1881, his stepson, Dr. A.G. Tillman Sr., erected a brick building on the site that housed the state's first telephone exchange.

Some thought local photographer J. Mack Moore looked like Mark Twain; in addition to a physical resemblance, Moore also loved the Mississippi River and steamboats. Moore was born in 1870, the year of the great race between the Lee and the Natchez. (CF.)

The only private home within the siege lines to survive the shelling in 1863, the Shirley House was almost lost to the elements. It was saved and completely restored when the Park was established in 1899. (JMM.)

Known as the Wheeler House in antebellum days, the building was later converted into the Vicksburg Infirmary, a leading medical facility. Sold in the 1970s, it was demolished to make way for an annex to First Baptist Church. (JMM.)

When A.B. Reading built this house in the 1830s, it was called Reading's Folly. It was later bought by the city and used as a hospital. It was used as a Confederate hospital and then a Yankee hospital after the siege, and later, it became Kuhn Hospital, a state facility. To the right is the Confederate annex, which burned in 1918. (JMM.)

Dedicated in 1880, King Solomon Missionary Baptist Church began as a mission in 1859 and was formally organized in 1866 as Mount Pleasant Church. The congregation changed the name to King Solomon in 1869. (JMM.)

The first St. Aloysius School building was constructed in the late 1880s at the corner of Grove and First North Streets and was called St. Aloysius College. The boys' school was operated by the Brothers of the Sacred Heart, who lived on the top floor. Classrooms were on the first and second floors, and the cafeteria and kitchen were in the basement.

Vicksburg firemen show off a fine Ahrens Fire Engine used by the men at Washington Fire House No. 3 in the 1870s. Posing with the engine in front of the Crawford Street station are, from left to right, as follows: Albert Loyd, foreman; Dan Johnson, driver; and Jake Voeinkle, engineer.

Henry Schlottman Transfer Company had the first large delivery truck in Vicksburg. It is shown parked here, in front of the Bock Fischel Dry Goods Company. Schlottman advertised piano moving and also had a warehouse, or storage rooms.

The elegant home of Lawrence Warner stood at the corner of Cherry and Crawford Streets until it was demolished in the 1950s and a service station was built on the site. Today, it is a parking lot. Warner was co-owner of Warner and Searles, a clothing store for men.

St. Paul Catholic Church, built in 1849 at Walnut and Crawford Streets, was located next door to the Baptist church. The priests' home (left) was built after the War Between the States. The church was damaged by cannon fire; a shell exploded through the sanctuary during Mass. The building was demolished after it was damaged by the tornado in 1953. (JMM.)

Men dressed in female attire, some carrying trumpets and some with onions on sticks that resembled batons, appear to be ridiculing the women's suffrage movement. The large man (kneeling) wears two ribbons, one reading "Onion Judge" and the other "Baton Rouge," and the number 199. (JMM.)

The old North house, later the home of the Randolph family, stood at the corner of Locust and Randolph Streets until it was destroyed by the 1953 tornado. The joists and beams were pinned with wooden pegs. The house was used as a tavern in 1940.

Streets paved with brick or other materials greatly improved travel in Vicksburg. This delivery truck of the Seale-Lily Ice Cream Company on south Washington Street could hardly have maneuvered the mud streets a few years earlier.

Originally the Wilson home, this house was later the Nogales Club. It was torn down in the 1930s and is now the site of Waring's Service Station. The house was hit at least 18 times during the siege. A Confederate soldier was buried in the garden. (HJH.)

McDonald and Miller provided the truck for the Boy Scouts to mount their scrap drive in 1938.

Fisher Funeral Home was located in the building on the right from c. 1880 until c. 1940. It was located on Grove Street, opposite the Old Court House, and served as Berea Baptist Church for a while. It later burned and was replaced by a modern office building. The man in the wheelchair is Frank J. Fisher. The house next door is the home of John and Vicki Barnes. (JMM.)

Come winter or high water, these residents were prepared with their cabin high off the ground and fireplace wood on the porch. Note the fine dove-tailing of the logs to the right and the plow stored under the house until springtime planting. (JMM.)

Snow blankets the Harding home on Chambers Street in this undated photo. (JMM.)

The Main Street School was built in the 1880s where the Vicksburg City Auditorium now stands. An earlier school had been operated by Prof. W.S. Young, who refused to take the loyalty oath after the surrender, and saw his property destroyed by the Union army. (JMM.)

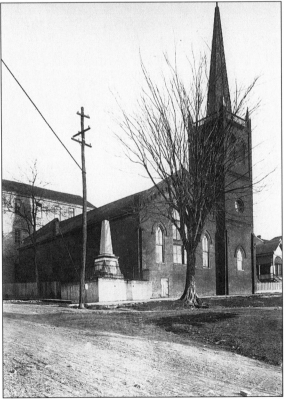

In 1828, Vicksburg Presbyterians erected this church at the corner of Monroe and First East Streets; it was later sold to Bethel A.M.E. and a new building was constructed on the site in 1912. The monument, relocated to Openwood Street, was erected by the City in memory of Dr. Hugh Bodley, who was killed by gamblers in 1835. (JMM.)

Anchuca, built *c.* 1830, was the first columned mansion in Vicksburg. Note the portion of the front porch enclosed with wire screens in the early 1900s. (JMM.)

Vicksburg's new city hall was completed in 1902 at the corner of Walnut and Crawford Streets. In later years, the porches were enclosed, and during the tornado of 1953, the heralds atop the building disappeared. (JMM.)

The rider and donkey are unidentified, but a pen-and-ink drawing of this photo was used in the following 1890 advertisement: "I lived 108 years, drank 78 barrels of whiskey, never got sick until I died, and bought my liquors at J.C. Moore's Jug House, Vicksburg, Miss." (JMM.)

South Street. Vicksburg, Miss.

Joe. Fox Carroll Hotel. Vicksburg. Miss. Publishe

The Browns lived in this home *c.* 1910 on the corner of South and Cherry Streets. The lot was originally part of the back yard of the Balfour House. The home was demolished to make way for business construction.

A lone figure, well-wrapped, trudges through the snow in front of the Willis home on Cherry Street in this 1919 snowscape. (JMM.)

Vicksburg looked like a winter wonderland when a heavy snow inundated the city in 1919. A car is parked on the street, as a trolley made its way slowly through the slush. The picture was taken near the front of the Willis home, close to the corner of Cherry and South Streets. (JMM.)

The home of Gov. Alexander G. McNutt, built in the 1820s, is one of the oldest houses in Vicksburg. It is now a private school. (JMM.)

The viaduct spanning the railroad tracks on Cherry Street was begun in 1910; this photo was taken November 20, 1910. (HJR.)

Baptists, who organized in Vicksburg in 1840, worshiped in a variety of buildings at the corner of Walnut and Crawford Streets before moving to their present structure. Their 1878 building was remodeled in 1906, expanding the outer walls and the tower. The structure burned in 1956.

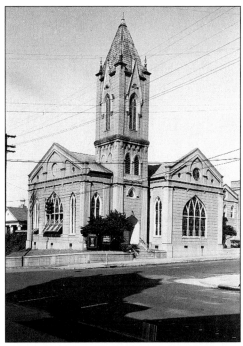

During the siege, the Yankees shelled the Baptist church so severely that it had to be reconstructed after the war; they shot off its steeple, which housed a 500-pound bell. The above structure was built in 1878 after the earlier one burned. (JMM.)

Freshly washed clothes hang in the sunshine as two men relax on the porch. (JMM.)

This cottage at the southeast corner of South and Walnut Streets was the home of Prof. Thomas Talen, a Vicksburg artist and musician in the late 1800s. The site is now occupied by commercial and government buildings. The Mahala Birchett house (background) was demolished in 1969 for parking spaces for the post office. One of the boys is Limerick McRae; the others are unidentified. (JMM.)

The National Park Store, located just east of the Illinois Memorial Temple, was operated by Mr. and Mrs. Z.M. Davis. Here, visitors could buy genuine artifacts from the siege as well as postcards, gasoline, and Delaware Punch. Mr. Davis, wearing a hat, is seen on the left of the group. (JMM.)

This house at the corner of Monroe and Crawford Streets, built in 1858, was the telephone exchange when this photo was taken on May 8, 1915. The first exchange was opened January 10, 1881, with 77 subscribers. A private line was put into operation on January 16, 1879, between the Cotton Exchange and the Anchor Lines elevator.

Washington Green, who was once president of the Board of Police before the War Between the States, had fallen on hard times when he discovered the remains of a mastodon on the outskirts of Vicksburg in 1879. He built a shed over his discovery and charged people to see the remains. Green, who lived off Hall's Ferry Road, became known as the "Halls Ferry Hermit." (JMM.)

A mule pulls this two-wheel cart driven by a wood merchant near the river. Woodyards were maintained all along the river to supply fuel for steamboats. (JMM.)

Cherry Street looked pretty bleak when this 1876 photo was taken from the top of the Old Court House. In the foreground is the Foose Building on the corner of Grove and Cherry; the top floor was destroyed by a tornado in 1953, and in recent years, the lower portion has been a laundry, a flower shop, and then a museum. Down the street is the Jewish temple, shown before the steeples were added. A brick wall, painted white, surrounded the jail. Beside it is the Featherstun house. (HJH.)

Before W.C. Craig built a Tudor-style home on Cherry Street (near the Belmont Street intersection) in the early 1900s, the home of John Wesley Vick stood there. A son of the city's founder, he was a Jefferson County native and graduate of Transylvania University in Kentucky. He developed a fine strain of cotton seed. The house was used as a Union hospital following the siege. (JMM.)

Little Will Klein is the only male in this cluster of females. From left to right are as follows: (front row) Janie McCutcheon, Shelby Thaxton Klein, Nellie Flanagan, Mary Lee Thaxton, and Janie Lea; (back row) Lucy Thaxton, Mary Brooke, Dolly Baggett, Lucy McCutcheon, Irma Thompson, and Carrie Belle Keykendall.

The occasion for this photograph is unknown, as are the individuals, including the little boy with his back turned, mooning the photographer! (JMM.)

Pres. William Howard Taft was entertained in this parlor in the old Elks Club building in 1908. The handsome, columned edifice stood on Walnut Street; it burned and was rebuilt. The second structure was demolished when a new clubhouse was built south of town. The site is now a parking lot.

The Mississippi River was a solid mass of ice on February 12, 1899, and the temperature was 10 below zero. The *Vicksburg Evening Post* noted that the ice was attracting "considerable attention, as it is a sight rarely witnessed by our citizens." The river again froze in January 1940. (AB.)

Oxen pull wagons up the Clay Street hill in the Hoffman Block, probably *c.* 1900. The corner of the Carroll Hotel, built in October 1893, is on the left. The house in the middle of the photo was demolished in 1907 and the First National Bank was built on the site. (AB.)

A wooden cutout of Abraham Lincoln pointed to the "Abe Lincoln Unique Tourist Court" on South Washington Street in the late 1940s. In the background is a log replica of the Lincoln birthplace in Kentucky. Owner N.W. Thayer, who dressed like Lincoln, advertised his tourist court as "Honestly the Best Night's Rest in the South" and claimed hot baths, kitchenettes, private garage, no noise, no dust, and gas heat.

Though it looked like an old country store with metal advertising signs, J. Lee Black and Son Groceries was located in town, on the corner of Cherry but facing Fayette Street. The photo was taken on August 8, 1929. Black and his wife, Anna, lived a few blocks away, on Main Street. (JBU.)

Iron-front stores such as these, located in the American National Bank building at the corner of Washington and Clay Streets, were typical of many downtown structures in the early 1900s. The bank was unique in that it had a female president, Mrs. Betty Willis. (JMM.)

An 1889 photo shows the interior of Crawford Street Methodist Church. The occasion for the floral decorations was probably a wedding. (JMM.)

Methodists built Crawford Street Church in 1848, and the brick structure with the tall dome was shelled in 1863 during the siege. It was demolished in 1899, and a new edifice was built on the site. The photo was taken in 1876, probably from the top of St. Paul Catholic Church. (HJH.)

In 1884, Crawford Street Methodist Church underwent extensive renovation and the domed tower was removed.

William H. Bruser, roofer and plumber, couldn't have asked for a better advertisement than the mansard roof on his own house on Washington Street. Next door was the Thomas A. Marshall house. This photo was taken in 1876. (HJH.)

Though in plain view of the river, the Thomas A. Marshall house went through the siege unscathed. The house burned in the 1880s. The terraced hill was graded in later years, and a service station was built there. A railroad tunnel runs beneath a corner of the property.

First Presbyterian Church was built on the corner of Cherry and South Streets in 1908 on the site of the home of Sen. Walker Brooke.

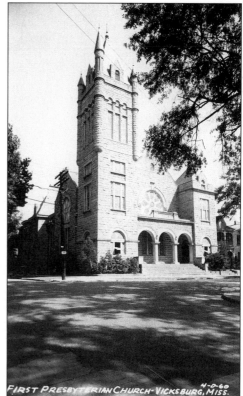

At the age of 95, Caroline Purnell Searles wrote her reminiscences of the War Between the States. After 40 years, she still called the Yankee soldiers "hirelings," as she said they fought for money, not for patriotism. She claimed the enemies' sentiments were "outrageously vandalistic from the beginning to the end of the conflict."

FIRST PRESBYTERIAN CHURCH-VICKSBURG, MISS.

Despite the gutters on each side, South Street was a muddy mess when this photo was taken in 1876. Note the sign reading "Grocery" on the shack (foreground) and the signs for the Vicksburg Boarding House and the A.M. Paxton and Company Foundry. (HJH.)

Two
WHEN COTTON WAS KING

If there's any doubt about it—that cotton was king in Vicksburg and Warren County—the big arch made of cotton bales on Washington Street was a reminder, especially to visiting Presidents William McKinley and Theodore Roosevelt.

In 1860, Mississippi produced more than a fourth of the nation's cotton crop, and despite war and destruction of the South's economy, the white fluffy staple had once again claimed its throne by the late 1800s. After the fields were prepared and plowed, seeds were planted, plants were hoed, and the mature bolls were picked. Wagons loaded to the gills creaked over country roads to the gins, where machines removed the seeds and the bolls were compressed into bales, each wrapped in burlap and weighing 400 to 500 pounds.

Vicksburg was the hub of the wheel of the cotton kingdom. Bridges were built across the Big Black and the Yazoo Rivers, connecting the main arteries from the rural areas so that farmers would find it easier to get to market. When steamboats pulled away from the wharf, their decks barely skimming the water, it made one wonder how they could float.

The cotton crop translated into jobs, prosperity, clothing, food, education, and homes. The basis of the economy and the backbone of society was cotton. Three bales of it were emblazoned on the seal of the City of Vicksburg. Cotton was king.

Arches of cotton bales were built on Washington Street when Presidents McKinley and Roosevelt came to town. (JMM.)

Though harvesting today is usually done by machine, these men were photographed c. 1950 picking it the old-fashioned way—by hand. (CF.)

Mules pulled wagons laden with cotton from all over central Mississippi and Louisiana to Vicksburg for ginning, baling, and shipping. In the 1890s, bridges were built over the Big Black and roads were improved, making the city easily accessible for those who lived in remote areas.

After the fields had been prepared, the seeds planted, the young plants "chopped," and the bolls picked, the final step before cotton was shipped to market was going to the gin. Plantation gins often served farmers of small crops in the community. (JMM.)

Holding large baskets of cotton, workers climb the steps at this rural gin. It took about 500 pounds of ginned cotton to make a bale, which was wrapped in burlap and bound by metal straps. (JMM.)

Wagons at harvest time wait their turn at one of the larger gins in Vicksburg. (JMM.)

Eight mules pull a wagon loaded with 15 bales of cotton up China Street hill (at the intersection with Monroe) *c.* 1900. (JMM.)

Wagons loaded with cotton line this Vicksburg street *c.* 1900, slowly making their way to the gin. A few wagons in the foreground already have their baled cotton. (JMM.)

The famous steamboat, *Robert E. Lee*, was built in 1866 in Indiana for the Vicksburg to New Orleans trade; it took on its first shipment of cotton at Vicksburg. The *Lee* was dismantled in 1876 and became a wharfboat at Vicksburg, and the *Robert E. Lee II* was built.

Cotton bales stacked on the wharf await loading aboard the *Natchez* in this 1876 photograph. (HJH.)

The *Natchez*, the eighth boat by that name, is docked at Vicksburg *c.* 1900, awaiting its cargo. The vessel was the only *Natchez* that was a sternwheeler. The captain was Blanche Leathers. (JMM.)

Roustabouts roll bales of cotton up the planks to the deck of the *Tennessee Belle*, which was the last steam packet on the lower Mississippi. She sank between Lake Providence and Vicksburg February 3, 1936. The boat was recovered, but it burned a few miles south of Natchez in November 1942. (JMM.)

The *F. Barksdale* was built in 1884 and operated on the Yazoo River by the Parisot line; she burned at Hendeick's Landing on December 13, 1888. (JMM.)

The *Katie Robbins* operated on the Yazoo River in the late 1800s, hauling cotton to Vicksburg. (JMM.)

The largest shipment of cotton ever made was aboard the *Henry Frank*, when she transported 9,226 bales in 1881. In addition, she had 250 tons of other freight aboard. The boat burned north of New Orleans at Davis Creek Island in 1884. (JMM.)

Three
ERAS OF STEAM & STEEL

Before it jumped the tracks, killing a sleeping wino whose time and place to doze had been ill-chosen, and demolishing Orbach's Saloon, the trolley was known by its number, 66. After this tragically memorable day in the early 1900s, it was forever called "Carrie Nation."

Trolleys were the favorite way to travel around town, but both steamboats and trains offered more luxurious travel. Train tracks weren't always steel, and trolleys weren't always electric. The earliest railroads that stretched out of Vicksburg had wooden rails, and the first trolleys were pulled by mules.

Steamboats had crowded the waterfront since Vicksburg's inception. They transported passengers and cargo from North to South and back again. In the 1840s, the first Sultana received a contract to carry the mail on a round trip from Vicksburg to New Orleans each week; soon others wanted aboard the gravy train, or in some cases, the "gravy boat." The most famous boats were known by the individual sounds of their whistles, and both trains and boats had bells and whistles and steam engines that hissed and sighed. In the late 1850s, another noise penetrated the waterfront when the steamboat *Amazon* came into port with its calliope playing. A "gosh-awful screech" was the way editor Marmaduke Shannon of the *Whig* described the music of the steam organ.

Steamboats brought famous visitors to town on such vessels as the *Grand Republic* and the *Fanny Bullitt*; in later years, they came by train.

Asphalt hasn't completely covered all the trolley tracks on Vicksburg's streets, and there are a few steamboats today, their whistles and calliopes beckoning those who long for a taste of nostalgia to come ride. An occasional train blows its warning as it approaches a crossing, but the eras of steam and steel are mostly remembered in the romance of history.

Competitors in delivery and transportation were trains and steamboats. Both are represented in this photo taken at the Vicksburg waterfront in the 1950s. (CF.)

The *Alice B. Miller*, built in Jeffersonville, Indiana, in 1904 was bought in 1908 by C.J. Miller of Vicksburg. She ran in the Yazoo and Sunflower Rivers trade and burned in 1915 at Vicksburg.

Built in 1887, the *Ben Hur* began operations in Pennsylvania, was next used as an excursion boat in Minnesota, and was then bought by Capt. Tom Morrisey of Vicksburg. She was owned by several others before she sank at Duckport in Madison Parish, Louisiana, in March 1916. (JMM.)

Open streetcars provided comfortable, breezy rides during the humid days of summer. During the winter, the sides were enclosed. The cars were electric; the earliest ones were pulled by mules. (JMM.)

Electric streetcars went into operation April 24, 1899, and operated until c. 1930, when a bus company began to provide city transportation. Some of the rails are still visible on city streets. The boy in the knickers (left) is Calvin Barber. (JMM.)

The engine that pulled the train into town in May 1901 was decorated with flags and bunting in honor of its famous passengers, Pres. and Mrs. William McKinley. They visited the National Cemetery before he gave a talk on Court Square. (JMM.)

This iron horse was a relic of the past when this photo was taken, probably in the early 1900s. (JMM.)

Rail lines led down into the water where trains were loaded on the *Pelican* for transfer between Mound, Louisiana, and Vicksburg in the early 1900s. After the bridge was built over the river in 1930, the *Pelican* was put into similar service between Friar's Point, Mississippi, and Helena, Arkansas. (JMM.)

The first of 15 cutoffs on the Mississippi River was begun in 1932 at Diamond Place, several miles south of Warrenton and above Davis Bend. This photo shows the dredge *George W. Catt* at work on the cutoff on November 13, 1932. The work was completed the following year, shortening the river by 10 miles.

A company operating a mule-drawn trolley system went into business in 1870 but soon abandoned its routes, only to resume when the electric streetcar company began to lay tracks. City workers tore up the tracks of the mule-drawn company and threw them away.

The electric trolley lines went into service in 1899, with eight miles of track and festivities including free rides, a barbecue for thousands, the observance of Confederate Memorial Day, and the erection of giant arches along the rail lines.

At night, electric lights called "the white way," illuminated the arches that had been built in celebration of the trolley car system.

Trolley tracks made a network of steel rails on the main thoroughfares; this scene is at the corner of Washington and Clay Streets. The trolley, Number 66, was nicknamed the Carrie Nation because it jumped the tracks and destroyed a saloon. (JMM.)

A trolley headed for Speed's Addition climbs the hill in front of the B.B. Club *c.* 1900, at the corner of Clay and Walnut Streets. (JMM.)

A silhouette of a race horse on the bow of the *Natchez* distinguished it as the vessel that raced the *Robert E. Lee* in 1870. Built in 1869, the *Natchez* had red smoke stacks between which hung a replica of a bale of cotton.

Most passenger steamboats provided fine dining and luxurious quarters. This one, the *S.S. Brown*, is shown in 1908. (JMM.)

Steamboats crowded the landing before the flood wall was built, and newspapers ran daily schedules for the various steamboat companies. Residents recognized the more famous steamers by their distinctive whistles, which could be heard for miles. (JMM.)

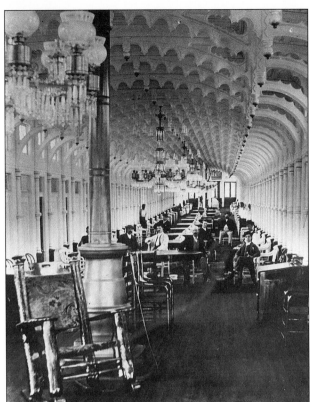

This massive chair was presented to Capt. T.P. Leathers of the *Natchez* in 1879 at Cincinnati, upon the launching of the vessel. The chair is now on display in the Old Court House Museum-Eva W. Davis Memorial in Vicksburg. (HJH.)

The *Sprague*, the largest steamboat ever built, was too big for the upper Mississippi, so it operated on the lower river. She shoved the largest tow in history—over 63,000 tons of coal. In 1948, she was sold to Vicksburg by Standard Oil Company and was converted into a museum. She burned in 1974. (CF.)

Four

A TRIBUTE TO VALOR

The horses came to a halt beneath the shade of a tree along the dusty road, and two old veterans got out of the buggy. One had worn gray, the other blue, almost a half century earlier.

"Stand here, General. Now turn that way just a little," one of them said to the other. "That's right where your statue will be and that's how it will look."

A year or so later, when the statue was dedicated, the old man wasn't there; he had died shortly after his visit to the site. He was Gen. Stephen Dill Lee, hero of Chickasaw Bayou and other Southern victories. Like the more famous Lee, after he sheathed his sword, he became an educator. The man with him had once been his enemy. Capt William T. Rigby was an Iowa veteran of the Vicksburg campaign. He had succeeded Lee as superintendent of the Vicksburg National Military Park.

The Park was established by Congress with Pres. McKinley signing the bill into law in 1899. Soon the Park began to take shape, a joint effort of historians and sculptors and engineers and contractors and politicians, their notions and ideas kept true by the old men who had endured the 47-day siege. They had been there; they remembered what happened.

"Here Brothers Fought," the inscription on the Pennsylvania memorial begins. These men had fought for principles. Today, plaques, statues, and monuments remind us of their heroism.

Confederate veterans and members of the family of Gen. Stephen D. Lee dedicated his statue in 1908. (JMM.)

Oxen pull a wagon, loaded with a boulder for the Massachusetts monument, down Jackson Street. (JMM.)

The Massachusetts monument was dedicated in 1903. It was the first in the Vicksburg National Military Park. (JMM.)

Children, each wearing a star, represented the 13 Confederate States when this statue of Pres. Jefferson Davis was dedicated in 1927. Davis is portrayed holding the Confederate flag and clutching a copy of the Constitution. The statue was sculpted by Henry Hudson Kitson. (JMM.)

It was Arkansas soldiers who sank the ironclad *Cincinnati* at Vicksburg in 1863, and it was a Confederate ironclad named *Arkansas* that played havoc with the Union navy in 1862. The Arkansas state memorial is inscribed with the motto, "A Nation Divided by the Sword and Reunited at the Altar of Faith."

The Alabama monument, dedicated in 1951, represents a "death stand" of Alabama troops, their heroism inspired by a woman who represents the state. Sculpted by Steffen Thomas, the bronze-on-granite structure is the only one in the Park dedicated to both the men and women of the state.

Giant flags covered the Memorial Arch when it was dedicated October 18, 1920, on Clay Street. For years, it was symbolic to travelers, as U.S. 80 followed the street into downtown Vicksburg. (JMM.)

Cars were narrow enough so that two could easily pass through the arch in the 1920s at the same time; in later years, the structure was moved into the Park. The individuals standing beside the Studebaker are unidentified. (JMM.)

The Illinois Memorial Temple, a replica of the Pantheon, was dedicated October 26, 1906, at a cost of $194,423.92. Inside it, bronze tablets list the names of the 36,000 Illinois troops who fought in the siege of Vicksburg. (JMM.)

Visitors enjoy a ride through the Park in a fashionable touring car in the early 1900s. (JMM.)

In 1890, during a Blue-Gray reunion, Tom Lewis opened the cave he had lived in on Grove Street during the siege. The cave collapsed in later years. Lewis drew up the first petition asking Congress to establish the Park. (JMM.)

For many years, the road from Fort Hill to Vicksburg ran through the water at Mint Springs, but there was a narrow bridge across the creek for foot traffic. Shown in this c. 1900 photo is part of the wall around the National Cemetery (right). (JMM.)

Mississippi's monument was dedicated November 13, 1909. Bronze reliefs portraying scenes of courage, valor, and sacrifice were cast in Italy and added three years later. The 76-foot-high monument of Mt. Airy granite was the first Southern one in the Park. (JMM.)

Two flags, each measuring 12 by 14 feet, covered the Pennsylvania monument before the granite marker was unveiled March 24, 1906. The inscription reads as follows: "Here brothers fought for their principles, here heroes died for their country, and a united people will forever cherish the precious legacy of their noble manhood." (JMM.)

A statue of Gen. Lloyd Tilghman portrays the Maryland-born Confederate general when he was mortally wounded at Champion's Hill in 1863. The statue was sculpted by Frederick Sievers. (JMM.)

The barrel of a cannon was used to mark the site where Pemberton and Grant met in July 1863 to discuss surrender terms for the city. A marble shaft once marked the place but was removed because visitors began taking chips as souvenirs. (JMM.)

A cannon from the *Cairo* and the pilot house were among the first items brought to the surface when efforts were made to raise the Union vessel. Since the ship was sunk by the Confederacy, it was deemed appropriate to fly the flag.

Crowds lined the bank of the Yazoo River each day during efforts to raise the *Cairo* in 1964. The vessel, now on display in the Park, was sunk in 1862 by Confederates. (ALG.)

Five

TRAGEDIES & TRIBULATIONS

The time was 5:35 p.m. on December 5, 1953. The streets were decorated with Christmas tinsel and wreaths, and shoppers crowded the downtown stores. A few blocks off the main drag, children enjoyed the Saturday feature at the Saenger Theater. Later that evening, a football game was to planned to benefit Leo Puckett, a Jett High School player who had been injured. It was unseasonably warm, too warm for football. But it was just right for a tornado. In a matter of minutes, downtown and some residential areas were in shambles, including the theater. Killer winds had left 38 people dead and scores injured.

Where were you when the tornado hit? Everyone had a story, some of miraculous escapes that could be attributed only to sheer luck or the merciful hand of Providence.

There have been other disasters in the city's past. Floods along the river's low lands are usually measured by the one in 1927, when all of the Delta, from Memphis to Vicksburg in Arkansas, Louisiana, and Mississippi became one huge lake, and Vicksburg opened her doors and hearts to more than 10,000 refugees.

There was the Yellow Fever Epidemic of 1878 that claimed over a thousand lives in the area in just a few weeks, and the Washington Street fire of 1885 that virtually destroyed the business district and took 52 lives.

In each instance, people rallied together to help those in need and assist the less fortunate. Troubles brought out the best in everyone. These were Vicksburg's finest hours.

His dreams and hopes smashed, Joe Wing Sing sits among the debris that had been his grocery store before the tornado demolished it. (CF.)

Christmas decorations survived the killer winds that wrecked downtown Vicksburg when the tornado hit on Saturday evening, December 5, 1953. (BEB.)

Little remained standing. It appears there was nothing worth salvaging in this scene of downtown Vicksburg. (BEB.)

Washington Street, the main business section, suffered mass destruction. Some buildings, however, such as The Valley, sustained little damage. (BEB.)

Taking a direct hit, the Saenger Theater on Walnut Street was wrecked. The falling debris killed a number of children who had gone to the Saturday matinee. (BEB.)

The tornado was no respecter of homes; it wrecked fine old mansions as well as humble abodes. This scene was taken on Locust Street. The Laughlin home is in the background. (BEB.)

None of the damage to the Old Court House was structural. The building had survived Yankee shelling and almost a century later, withstood a tornado. Here, A.S. Davis has climbed to the cupola to wave the Confederate flag. (CF.)

The levee provided refuge for both man and beast during this flood. (JMM.)

Sandbagging did not keep the flood waters away from the waterfront in the early 1900s. (JMM.)

Goats take refuge from the flood waters on the roof of a barn. (JBU.)

The steamboat *Tollinger* brought a load of sick refugees to Vicksburg in April 1927. (JBU.)

Water was up to the floorboards of this truck in front of Ryan's Coal Yard on north Washington Street *c.* 1922.

A truck laden with cases of Coca-Cola pulls through water that surrounded the depot *c.* 1920. (JMM.)

These volunteers were among the many who worked with the Red Cross to alleviate the suffering and provide for victims of the flood of 1927. In the background are tents for the refugees. (JMM.)

Dr. Sylvan D. Myers helped inoculate the refugees against disease. (JBU.)

Illinois Central Railroad Company employees work desperately to hold back the water in 1916. (JMM.)

Workers sandbag around the Yazoo and Mississippi Valley Railroad Depot in 1922.

There was a funeral service in progress when the bottom literally fell out of King David M.B. Church on Bowmar Avenue in 1912. Despite the magnitude of the collapse, there were few injuries.

Though the floor had fallen, the walls and roof of King David held, which probably prevented some fatalities. The building was erected on tall brick piers.

Six
REMEMBERING THE
GOOD TIMES

"Seventy-six trombones led the big parade . . ." Well, maybe not that many, but Vicksburg did love a parade, and it didn't take much excuse to stage one. There were the parades the circus held, showing off their elephants and clowns, enticing the curious to come to the big top, and there were the school bands, usually with a fat little boy struggling with a tuba. Parades, complete with bunting on the buildings and gaily decorated carriages, honored the famous, such as Teddy Roosevelt. Occasionally, the LSU Special would stop on its way to a football game long enough for Louisiana's flamboyant governor, Huey Long, all decked out in his white suit, to lead the Tigers' marching band down Washington Street.

The city celebrated not only when the famous came, but also for the opening of the Yazoo Canal, when the town staged its centennial, and when Bloom's Fountain was dedicated. There were elaborate plans for the Flower Parade (there wasn't room for another posey on a float), and the filming of *The Crisis* created an impromptu gathering by the hundreds.

Folks turned out to watch the Volunteer Southrons and to hear them in concert on Court Square. There were fish frys, watermelon cuttings, and ice cream socials. Vicksburgers cheered their baseball team, the Billies. Women enjoyed afternoon teas or bridge parties; men liked poker and beer. The admonition about "all work and no play" did not go unheeded.

The band was all male, as was St. Aloysius until the mid-1900s. The Catholic school began as a commercial college.

Men enjoy a friendly game aboard the *Annie Laurie*. (JMM.)

The time, place, and participants are unknown, but it looks like party time. (JMM.)

Butterflies appear to propel this float in the Flower Parade in 1916. Because World War I began the next year, the parade was discontinued. (JMM.)

Metzger, "The Shoe King," featured a boot in the Flower Parade. While most floats were motorized, this one was pulled by a horse and buggy. (JMM.)

It's watermelon time! (JMM.)

Fishermen dress their catch in this undated photo. (JMM.)

Mandolin players and violinists dominated this youthful orchestra, probably in the 1920s, though there were also four members in the brass section and one in percussion. Note the girls' hair styles and the boys' knickers. (JMM.)

The Volunteer Southrons band performed at the dedication of the Confederate monument in Soldiers' Rest Cemetery in April 1893. They are, from left to right, Albert Auter, Kirk Bond, Frank Groome, John Piazza, George Kelly Smith, Abe Katzenmeyer, Willie Katzenmeyer, Felix Mahen, John Burnhardt, Vic O'Conner, Vick Fisher, Fred Moser (director), Dennis Hossley, John G. Katzenmeyer, Tip Brunnar, and Lee Spengler. (JMM.)

Vicksburg's royalty, chosen to reign over the city's centennial celebration in 1925, are shown arriving at the landing aboard the steamboat *Charles Miller* on May 15, 1925. Leading the procession are Dick Jones and Ruth Blanks.

Children from the congregation of St. George Orthodox Church were participants in a "Tom Thumb Wedding," sponsored by the Cedars Ladies Club *c.* 1940. (CF.)

The Volunteer Southrons stand at attention, ready to parade. The photo was taken at the corner of Washington and Clay Streets c. 1900. One sign was for the store of Henry Yoste, a jeweler and watchmaker; the one on the awning reads "Saw Mill Office." Next door was the Garden Restaurant. (JMM.)

The dedication of Bloom's Fountain on Monroe Street was held in 1927. The fountain, bequeathed to the city by Louis Bloom, features the Greek goddess Hebe, who typifies eternal youth and joyousness. (JMM.)

When the *Belle of the Bends* docked in October 1907, Pres. Theodore Roosevelt was on board. Citizens rushed to greet him and then filled the hills on Court Square to hear him speak. (JMM.)

Sen. John Sharp Williams (standing) introduced Theodore Roosevelt at the Old Court House in 1907. Sitting to the right of Senator Williams is Gen. Stephen D. Lee, and next to him is Roosevelt. After his return to Washington, the president's family visited Vicksburg. (JMM.)

A dredge works in the old river bed, helping to construct the Yazoo Diversion Canal. It was completed in 1902, once again giving Vicksburg a waterfront. The Mississippi River changed course in 1876; after this, steamboats could come to the old landing only during high water.

A parade of steamboats with the *Senator Cordill* in the lead celebrated the opening of the canal. (JMM.)

The Mississippi Division of the United Confederate Veterans were joined by members of the United Daughters of the Confederacy for this parade. The car is parked in front of the Elks Club on Walnut Street. (JMM.)

Crowds gather for a parade on Washington Street, near the intersection with Clay in the early 1900s. A sign on the horse in the center reads "Past and Present."

Children carrying floral wreaths participated in the dedication of the Confederate monument in 1893.

When Pres. and Mrs. William McKinley toured Vicksburg May 1, 1901, they rode in a gaily decorated carriage driven by Charles Schuler. A Union army veteran, McKinley won Southern hearts when he paid tribute to the Confederate flag. (AB.)

The cause of the celebration is unknown, but the bandstand in the National Cemetery was decorated with small U.S. flags. Many of the ladies and men pose with floral arrangements for this late 1800s photo.

The ladies in this photo called their organization "The Five O'clock Club." It was probably purely social and presumably met at five o'clock.

Bunting, flags, and a portrait of William McKinley decorate the Tillman building on the corner of Washington and Clay Streets. Several people get a bird's-eye view from the roof.

When the B'Nai B'rith Literary Association building was completed in March 1917, the dedication celebration included a grand ball. (JNH.)

Vicksburg's first country club building was located on Mulvihill near Drummond. The only person identified is B.W. Griffith, who is wearing the white suit. He was president of the First National Bank and mayor of Vicksburg.

Enthusiastic and curious movie fans crowd the courthouse hill in 1916 to watch the Selig Polyscoe Company film a scene for the movie *The Crisis*. (JMM.)

Seven

A VISIT TO THE COUNTRY

It wasn't unusual for the newspaper, around 1900, to note that well-known citizens from out in the country were in the city on business. They came from Oak Ridge, Bovina, Redbone, Davis Bend, Newman's, Freetown, Possum Hollow, Eagle Bend, Nannachehaw, Eldorado, Glass, Redwood, Youngton, Newtown, and Yokena. They often spent the night before returning home, and it was often months before they made the trip again, for farm families were practically self-sufficient.

It was a special treat for city folks to visit the country. That's when and where grandchildren learned to ride horses, feed the chickens, milk a cow, swing on a grapevine, and go swimming in the creek.

Society in the country usually centered around the school, church, and general store. News was swapped at Sunday services or beside the stove at the community store, a place where you could buy everything from pills, plows, and petticoats to coffins and calico. School programs, always held to raise money, featured cake walks and box lunches. In the fall, there were protracted meetings at the churches with dinners on the grounds and baptizing in local ponds. During political campaigns, there were picnics at Yokena and Newman's Grove and Oak Ridge where folks went to eat, visit, and hear politicians' promises.

Country folks usually rose before day in order to get all the work done, but they would take time for fishing or just swinging on the front gallery late in the day.

A trip to the country was good for body and soul.

Buena Vista on Eagle Lake was built by Col. B.G. Kiger in 1856. This photo was taken in the 1920s. (JMM.)

Children help this woman as she feeds the chickens. (JMM.)

Boys in their Sunday best show off their prize-winning livestock, probably at the local fair. (JMM.)

Hog killing was a festive time on farms. Hogs provided bacon, ham, salt meat, sausage, cracklings, souse, lard, and chitterlings. In this photo, the carcass is being raised by block and tackle under a tree. (CF.)

Hot water was used to douse the carcass that had been scraped and gutted. Hog killing was always done on a very cold day because the meat might spoil in warm weather. The occasion ran a close second to Christmas as a time of celebration. (CF.)

Rendering lard during hog-killing time required the help of everyone, even the children. Charlie Faulk of the *Vicksburg Evening Post* wrote that workers would "chatter and chuckle . . . children would press for a better view . . . and dogs would sniff fearfully as they peered between the legs of spectators." (EWD.)

Bovina was an early stop on the stagecoach route before railroads were built, and John Cowan opened a tavern there in 1827. Bovina was a thriving rural village with a post office, school, churches, and stores when this photo was taken in the early 1900s.

The oldest church in Warren County, Redbone Methodist, was organized in 1814 east of Warrenton. The brick sanctuary, built in 1854, replaced early wooden structures. During the occupation of Vicksburg, it was used as a Union hospital. In 1917, the church burned. It was restored in 1947.

In the 1940s, country ladies operated a market in Vicksburg where they sold farm produce, flowers, and pastries. The president of the market for many years was Mrs. Carrie Lee Cotton of the Jeff Davis community. She is shown here in her starched white apron, displaying two baskets of farm-fresh eggs. (JP.)

Though a tranquil scene in the 1920s, Chickasaw Bayou was the site of a fierce battle and Southern victory in 1862. It is now considered "in town," but at the time of the skirmish, it was located north of the city. (JMM.)

Men, horses, and dogs appear to be ready for a hunt in this early 1900s view. (JMM.)

The hounds look hungry in this photo. The man sixth from the left is thought to be Holt Collier, who was a famous hunter, Confederate veteran, and guide for the Teddy Roosevelt bear hunt in 1902. (JMM.)

Men watch as mules pull a road-grading machine, probably in the early 1900s. At one time, property owners were responsible for the upkeep of roads. (JMM.)

Warren County supervisors pose with four new road-grading machines c. 1950. The only man identified is J.H. Henderson, who is standing and wearing a white suit.

The store at Yokena, owned by the Hankinson and Hyland families, was a landmark for decades. It served as a post office, plantation commissary, railroad stop, and general store. For years, it was operated by T.J. Kinzer and then by Jack and Susie Ogle. It burned in 1959. (GC.)

When Joe LaBatta, a young Italian immigrant arrived at Yokena in the 1880s, he went to work for the Hankinsons as a gardener, living in a small house behind the family home. This photo was taken in the late 1940s. LaBatta died in 1950 and was buried in the Yokena cemetery. (CF.)

The library at Hurricane Plantation on Davis Island became a home for the Joe Davis family after their house was burned in 1862 by Yankee soldiers. Sometimes called the Garden Cottage, the building faced the landing on the Mississippi. This photo was taken *c.* 1910. (JMM.)

A fire destroyed the Hurricane Library in 1919, and later that year, flood waters inundated the site. Only the columns remained, reflected in the water, designating where the house had been.

When J.H. Culkin Academy opened in 1916, it was one of five consolidated rural schools in Warren County. The others were Jefferson Davis, Jett, Bovina, and Oak Ridge. Designed by a Mr. Kramer, the buildings were identical. Each was dark green with white trim. (JMM.)

Long Lake, north of Vicksburg, was a peaceful setting when this picture was taken of a Miss Brown around the turn of the century. (JMM.)

The Willis house was located not far from Grant's headquarters and served as a Union hospital in 1863. To the right is the plantation gin. (AB.)

Oxen and mules have long been called "beasts of burden," used for centuries to help man. The individuals and the place are unidentified.

The congregation of Wayside Baptist Church in the Jeff Davis community posed for this photo on June 28, 1931, when the new sanctuary was dedicated. (JBU.)

Rev. William Wilson Bolls was ordained at Antioch Baptist Church in 1853 and returned to pastor the church in the 1890s, when this photo was taken. Bolls was a typical, old-fashioned country preacher. He served congregations for almost half a century.

Once a fine plantation home, the Messenger house stood near the banks of the Big Black River north of Bovina. During the War Between the States, all the furnishings were stolen by the Union army, but their actions were excused by General W.T. Sherman, who stated that anyone with that much furniture deserved to lose it. The house, long abandoned, was demolished *c.* 1960.

In 1897, when flood waters covered the lawn of the Freeland house south of Warrenton, the cows climbed above the flood to the front porch. Plantations owned by the Freelands, Hendersons, Adams, and Simralls were destroyed by the Diamond Point cutoff on the river in 1933.